MODERN ARBAN-ST. JACOME
Comprehensive Course for Cornet or Trumpet

THE *Modern Arban-St. Jacome*, a comprehensive course for cornet or trumpet, represents a compilation of two of the world's most famous cornet methods, completely revised, re-edited and re-styled to meet the demands of modern education. The original editions of these justly celebrated works, abounding in a wealth of valuable material that for over half a century proved itself indispensable in cornet study, were written at a time when teaching procedures were quite different from what they are today, and as a result, any attempt to make use of them in our present scheme of education inevitably results in a multitude of problems confronting students and teacher alike. Originally intended for pupils whose interests were paramount enough to justify them giving their full attention to music study, the original versions of these great works advance in strides far too rapid for most students. Furthermore, the material as presented in the original dress of these two methods is not graded progressively; the first pages of each book are of a difficulty far beyond most beginners, and when proceeding through the two methods it is found that while the musical content is easy enough to digest in some places, in others it is completely out of bounds for those at that particular stage of advancement. Furthermore, melodic material in the form of well-known melodies, which is so necessary in sustaining students' interest while developing the mere mechanical aspects of musical performance, hardly exists among the pages of either Arban or St. Jacome. These facts convinced the writer that time was opportune for a complete revision and adjustment of the two greatest of all cornet methods, in order to bring them to a place where they could be of some real service to the students of today as well as be adaptable to either individual instruction or the class method plan of teaching.

IN the present volume the writer has directed all efforts toward modernizing and improving the original versions of Arban and St. Jacome. Many new and worthwhile studies and exercises have been incorporated into the work, and in places, complete new sections have been added, given over to such problems as hitherto remained in the background. Many familiar melodies have been interspersed throughout the array of technical material, and each of the most frequently played major and minor keys is taken up in a systematic, logical fashion. Throughout the whole of *Modern Arban-St. Jacome*, constant stress is made of ' ' absolute necessity of (1) the regular practice of long in themselves of prime im *strength of lip muscles, a* interval and lip slurs, wh portance to all in developing flexibility

THE current work is admirably suited for class instruction in schools and its use therein will bring to the young musicians of America an opportunity to profit from the study of valuable teaching materials, devised and written by two of the greatest masters of the cornet that the world has ever known, but which have hitherto been inaccessible to a large number of students due to their former manner of presentation.

AS a companion book to the *Modern Arban-St. Jacome*, the writer has prepared a completely revised and modernized edition of the famous Pares exercises for trumpet (cornet), which is titled the *Modern Pares* and is published by Rubank, Inc. It is strongly urged that when students have studied as far as page 62 in the present work, they be introduced to the worthwhile scale and foundation studies of Pares, these two books being used in conjunction with one another from there on.

IF the *Modern Arban-St. Jacome* proves itself a boon to those in quest of material to aid in solving the many problems that confront the present day instructors of cornet (trumpet), whether they be private teachers of the instrument, or public school music directors, the writer will feel gratified to know that his earnest efforts have been of at least some educational significance.

Harvey S. Whistler, Ph. D.

Fingering Chart for Cornet or Trumpet

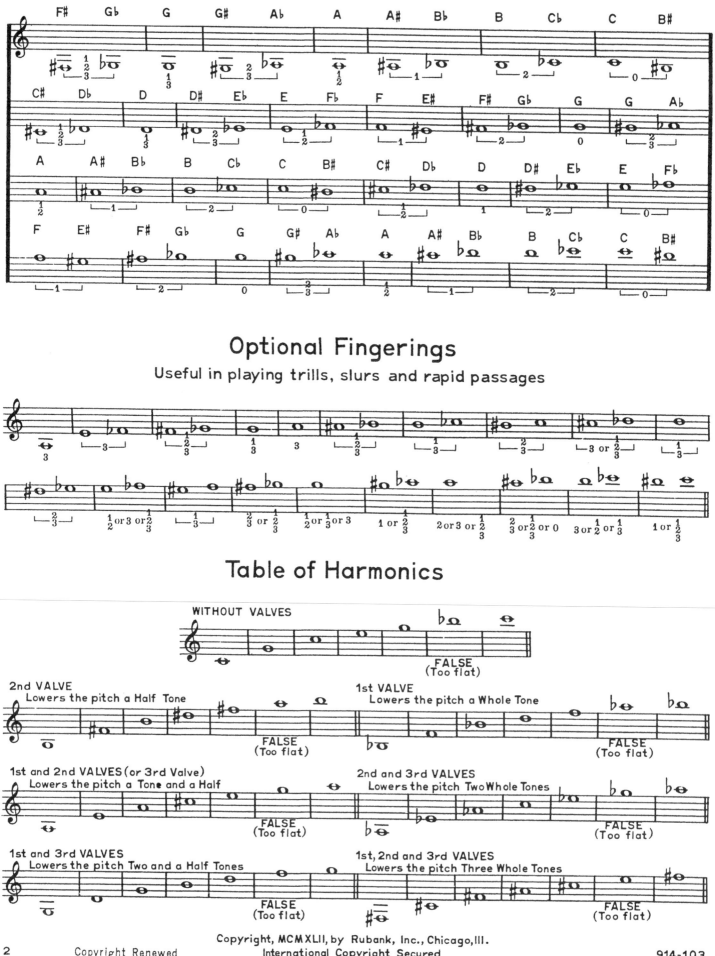

Optional Fingerings
Useful in playing trills, slurs and rapid passages

Table of Harmonics

914-103

Preliminary Lesson

Starting on "Middle C"
(For students finding it necessary to begin on this tone)

Whole Note (○) = Four Counts — Whole Rest (▬) = Four Counts

Preparatory Studies

THE FIRST TONES

Whole Note (o) = Four Counts — Whole Rest (𝄻) = Four Counts

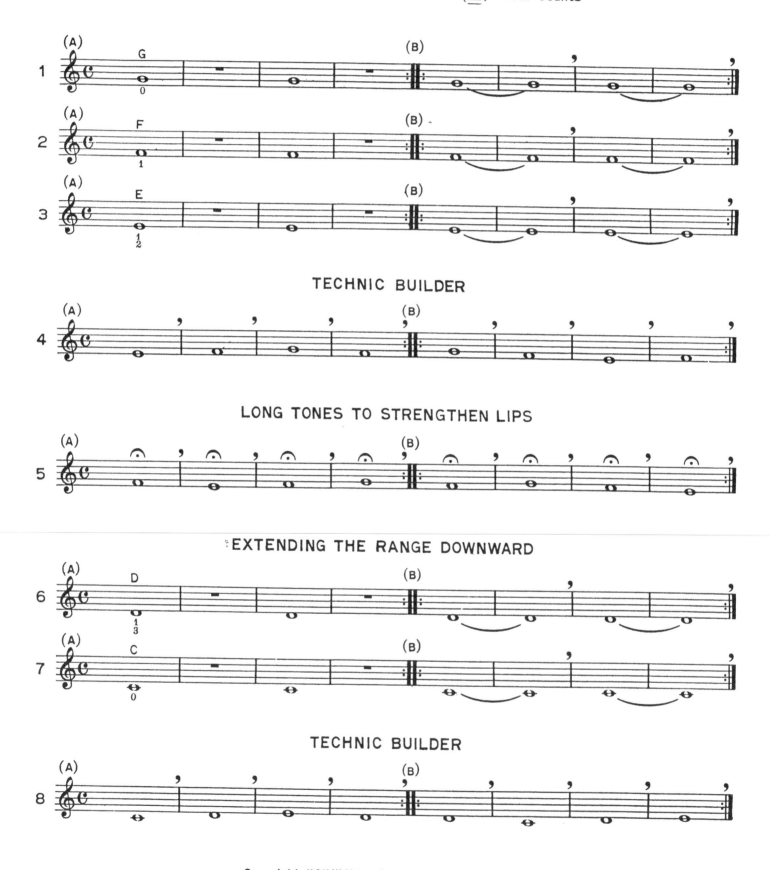

TECHNIC BUILDER

LONG TONES TO STRENGTHEN LIPS

EXTENDING THE RANGE DOWNWARD

TECHNIC BUILDER

Copyright, MCMXLII, by Rubank, Inc., Chicago, Ill.
International Copyright Secured

914-103

FOUNDATION STUDIES

INTRODUCING A NEW TONE

TECHNIC BUILDER

FOUNDATION STUDIES

LONG TONES TO STRENGTHEN LIPS

INTRODUCING HALF NOTES and HALF RESTS

Half Note (♩) = Two Counts — Half Rest (𝄼) = Two Counts

HALF NOTE EXERCISE

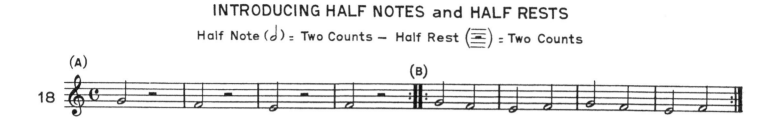

SLURS

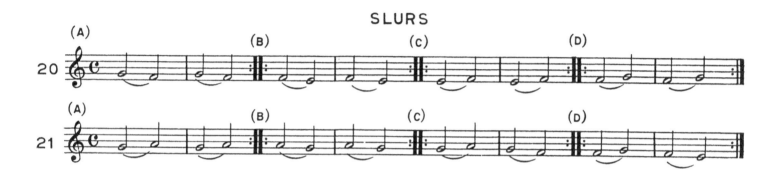

ANOTHER HALF NOTE EXERCISE

MORE SLURS

TONE BUILDER

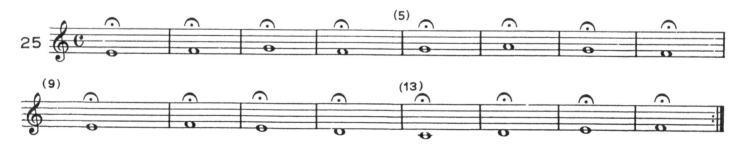

914-103

INTRODUCING QUARTER NOTES and QUARTER RESTS

Quarter Note (♩) = One Count — Quarter Rest (𝄽) = One Count

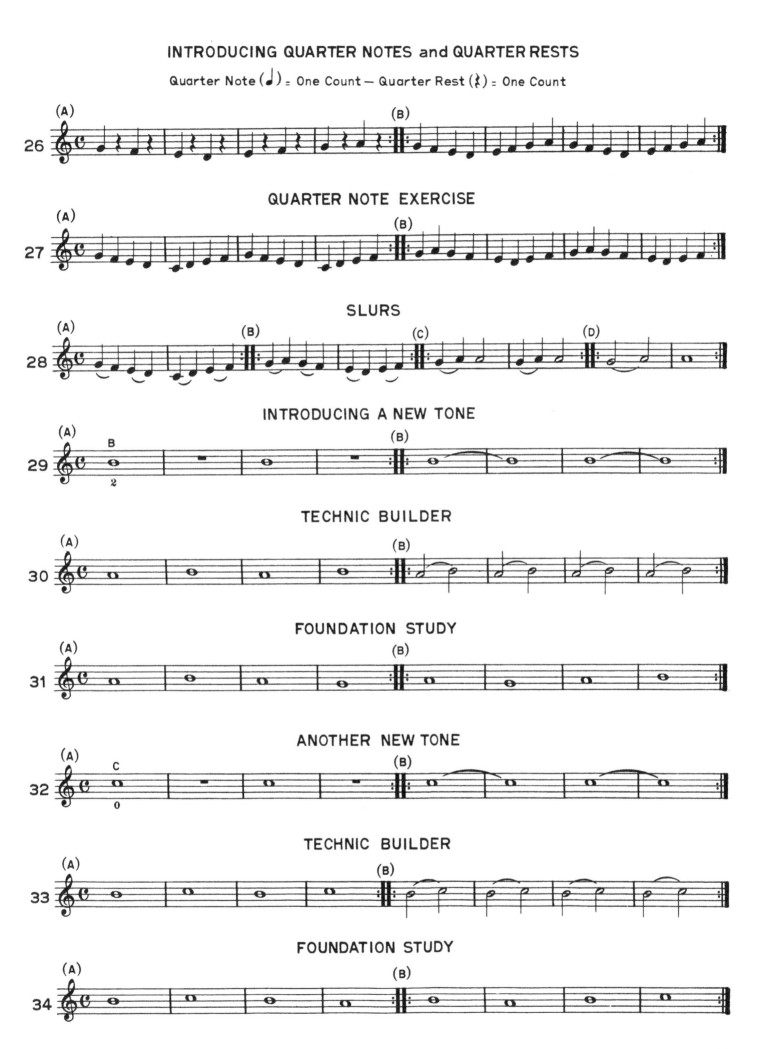

QUARTER NOTE EXERCISE

SLURS

INTRODUCING A NEW TONE

TECHNIC BUILDER

FOUNDATION STUDY

ANOTHER NEW TONE

TECHNIC BUILDER

FOUNDATION STUDY

TECHNIC BUILDER

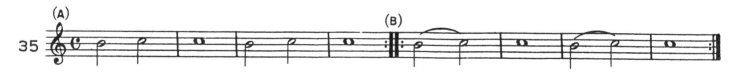

35

SLURS

36

37

TONE BUILDER

38

EXTENDING THE RANGE UPWARD

39

TECHNIC BUILDER

40

FOUNDATION STUDY

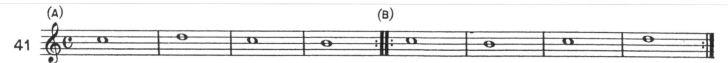

41

EXERCISE

42

TONE BUILDER

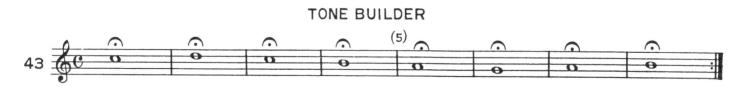

43

914-103

Favorite Melodies

LONG, LONG AGO

T. H. BAYLY

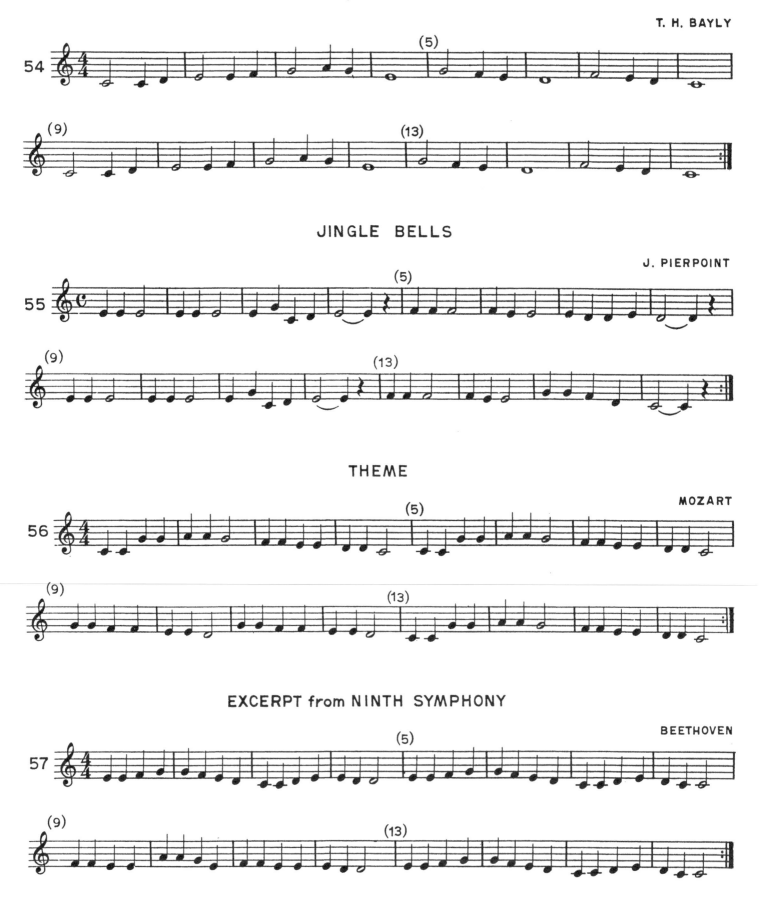

JINGLE BELLS

J. PIERPOINT

THEME

MOZART

EXCERPT from NINTH SYMPHONY

BEETHOVEN

914-103

GAILY THE TROUBADOR

T.H.BAYLY

WITH ALL THY HOSTS

from the Christmas Oratorio

BACH

FESTIVAL DAY

BALFE

MARTHA

von FLOTOW

Introducing ²⁄₄ Time (Meter)

EXERCISE

Introducing ¾ Time (Meter)

EXERCISE

Count 1 2 3

THE DOTTED HALF NOTE

♩. = Three Counts

WALTZ TIME

EMERALD WALTZ

Von BLON

Technical Studies

DEVELOPING LIP FLEXIBILITY AND STRENGTH

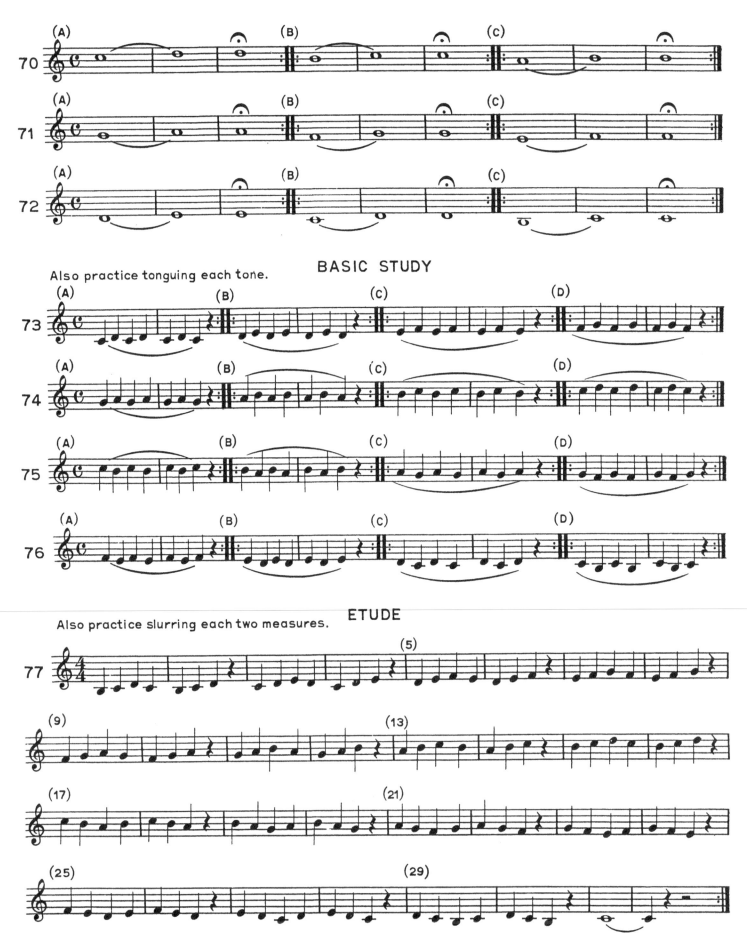

Also practice tonguing each tone.

BASIC STUDY

Also practice slurring each two measures.

ETUDE

914-103

Rhythmical Studies

INTRODUCING EIGHTH NOTES

Count 1 & 2 &

QUARTER AND EIGHTH NOTES ALTERNATED

Count 1   2 &

THE EIGHTH REST

Count 1 & 2 & 1 & 2 &

EIGHTH NOTES IN 4/4 TIME (Meter)

Count 1 & 2 & 3 & 4 &

TECHNIC BUILDER

FOUNDATION STUDY

Key of C Major

(A) Scale of C   (B) Chord of C

Also practice very slowly, holding each tone for (1) FOUR counts and (2) EIGHT counts.
When playing long tones, practice (1) $\prec$ and (2) $\prec\!\!\!\succ$.

SLURS

Also practice very slowly, holding each tone of each slur for FOUR counts.

DEVELOPING "E"

SCOTCH AIR

Moderato   Traditional

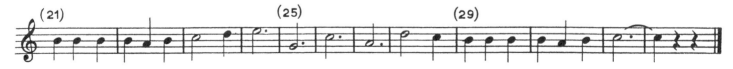

INTRODUCING THE DOTTED QUARTER NOTE FOLLOWED BY AN EIGHTH NOTE

OLD WELSH MELODY

Largo from New World Symphony

Key of F Major

(A) Scale of F   F   **(B)** Chord of F

92

Also practice very slowly, holding each tone for (1) FOUR counts and (2) EIGHT counts.
When playing long tones, practice (1) ◁ and (2) ◁ ▷.

SLURS

Also practice very slowly, holding each tone of each slur for FOUR counts.

93

PIONEER SONG

Con espressivo   Traditional

94

DEVELOPING "F"

95

96

Introducing ⅜ Time (Meter)

Count 1 2 3   12 3   1 2 3

THEME

W. B. BRADBURY

Larghetto

mp

p

Introducing ⅝ Time (Meter)

Count 1   2   3   4   5   6   12   3   45   6   1 2 3 4 5 6

Drink to Me Only With Thine Eyes

English Air

Cantabile

mp   *p*

mf

mp

Key of G Major

(A) Scale of G   (B) Chord of G

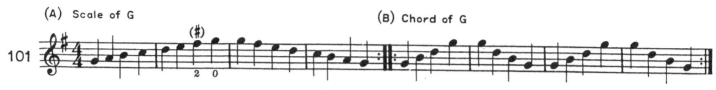

Also practice very slowly, holding each tone for (1) FOUR counts and (2) EIGHT counts.
When playing long tones, practice (1) ⫸ and (2) ⫸ ⫷

SLURS

Also practice very slowly, holding each tone of each slur for FOUR counts.

SHORT EXERCISES EMPLOYING "MIDDLE F♯"

(A)   (B)   (C)   (D)

On Wings of Song

Andante   MENDELSSOHN

rall.

ANDANTINO

LEMARE

DEVELOPING "F#"

DEVELOPING "G"

Melody from Oberon

WEBER

Key of B♭ Major

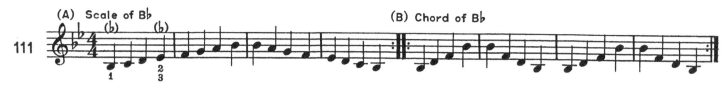

(A) Scale of B♭   **(B)** Chord of B♭

111

Also practice very slowly, holding each tone for (1) FOUR counts and (2) EIGHT counts.
When playing long tones, practice (1) ⎯⎯ and (2) ⎯⎯ ⎯⎯ .

SLURS

Also practice very slowly, holding each tone of each slur for FOUR counts.

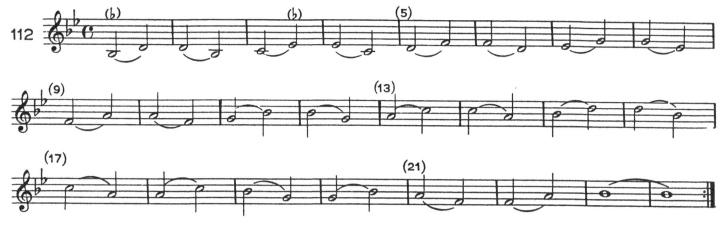

112

SHORT EXERCISES EMPLOYING "LOW B♭"

113

SONG WITHOUT WORDS

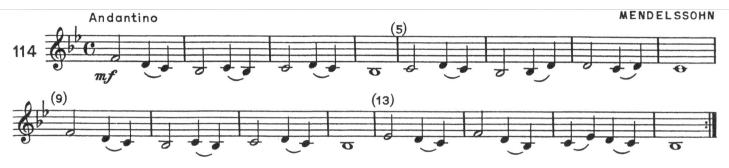

MENDELSSOHN

Andantino

114   *mf*

HANSEL and GRETEL

HUMPERDINCK

Con moto

115   *mf*

914-103

INTRODUCING "FOURTH SPACE E♭"

ADESTE FIDELIS

Grandioso

Traditional

ANVIL CHORUS

from Il Trovatore

VERDI

Maestoso

AULD LANG SYNE

Con energico

Scotch Folk Song

Key of D Major

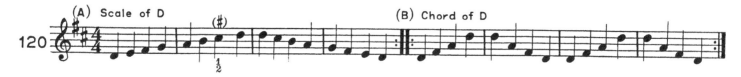

120 (A) Scale of D (B) Chord of D

Also practice very slowly, holding each tone for (1) FOUR counts and (2) EIGHT counts.
When playing long tones, practice (1) ⊂ and (2) ⊂ ⊃.

SLURS

Also practice very slowly, holding each tone of each slur for FOUR counts.

121 (5)

(9) (13)

(17) (21)

INTRODUCING "MIDDLE C#"

122 (A) (#) (B) (C) (D)

VALSETTE in D

Tempo di Valse   J. LEYBACH

123 (5)
mp

(9) (13)

FRENCH FOLK SONG

Con fervore   Traditional

124 (5)
mf

(9) (13)

914-103

INTRODUCING STACCATO

DEVELOPING THE STACCATO

STACCATO STUDY ON THE SCALE

STACCATO EXERCISE

EIGHTEENTH CENTURY THEME

MOZART

Key of E♭ Major

(A) Scale of E♭ (B) Chord of E♭

130

Also practice very slowly, holding each tone for (1) FOUR counts and (2) EIGHT counts.
When playing long tones, practice (1) ⟨ and (2) ⟨⟩

SLURS

Also practice very slowly, holding each tone of each slur for FOUR counts.

131

STACCATO EXERCISE ON THE SCALE

132

STACCATO STUDY

133

THEME from AMARYLLIS

H. GHYS

Brilliante

134

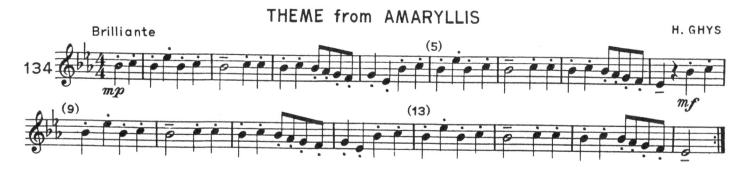

AIR from DER FREISCHUTZ

WEBER

Con ardore

135

Skater's Waltz

E. WALDTEUFEL

Grazioso

136

Swanee River

STEPHEN C FOSTER

Andante e semplice

137

Key of A Major

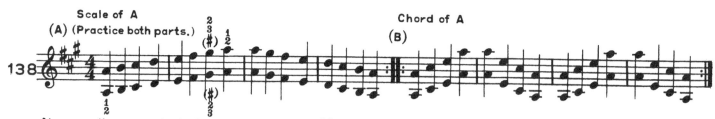

Scale of A
(A) (Practice both parts.)

Chord of A
(B)

138

Also practice very slowly, holding each tone for (1) FOUR counts and (2) EIGHT counts.
When playing long tones, practice (1) ⟨ and (2) ⟨⟩.

SLURS

Also practice very slowly, holding each tone of each slur for FOUR counts.

139

AMERICAN PIONEER SONG

Allegro

Traditional

140

DEVELOPING "LOW A"

141

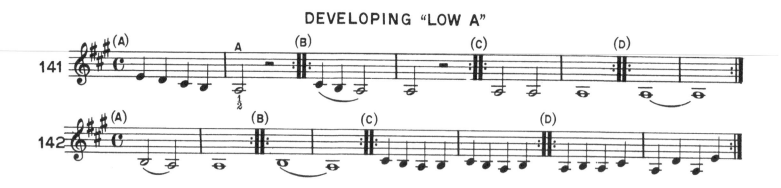

142

MELODY IN THE LOW RANGE

Moderato

W. B. BRADBURY

143

914-103

AURA LEE

Allegretto

Old Song

144

mf

(5)

(9)

(13)

EXCERPT from L'ARLESIENNE SUITE

Animato

BIZET

145

mf

(5)

(9)

(13)

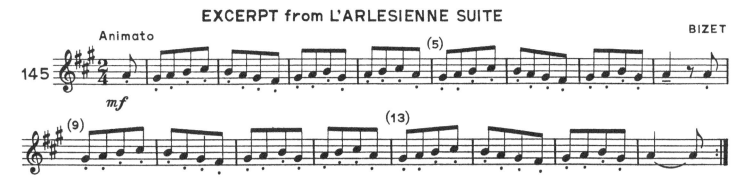

IMPROMPTU, Op. 142

Andante

SCHUBERT

146

mf

(5)

(9)

(13)

DEVELOPING "HIGH G#"

147

(A)

G#
2
3

(B)

(C)

(D)

148

(A)

(B)

(C)

(D)

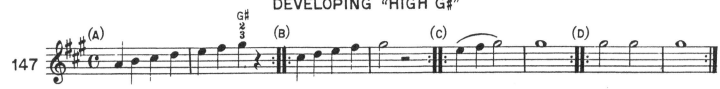

DEVELOPING "HIGH A"

149

(A)

A
1
2

(B)

(C)

(D)

150

(A)

(B)

(C)

(D)

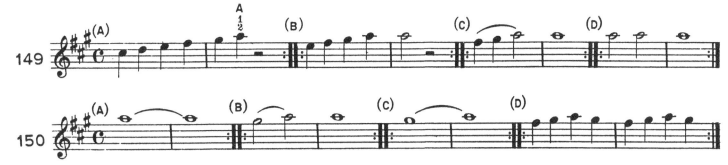

Key of A♭ Major

Scale of A♭
(Practice both parts.)

Chord of A♭

151

Also practice very slowly, holding each tone for (1) FOUR and (2) EIGHT counts.
When playing long tones, practice (1) ⟨ and (2) ⟨⟩.

SLURS

Also practice very slowly, holding each tone of each slur for FOUR counts.

152

GOLDEN SLIPPERS

Scherzando

JAMES A. BLAND

153

SHORT EXERCISES EMPLOYING "MIDDLE D♭"

154

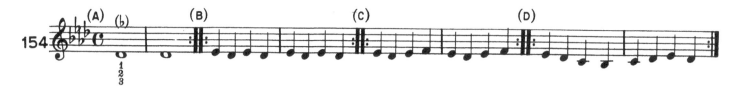

THEME

Commodo

J. LEYBACH

155

914-103

DEVELOPING "LOW Ab"

MELODY IN THE LOW RANGE

W.B. BRADBURY

SOLDIERS' CHORUS from FRA DIAVOLO

AUBER

STRENGTHENING "HIGH Ab"

PROCESSIONAL MARCH

HAYDN

Key of E Major

163

(A) Scale of E   (B) Chord of E

Also practice very slowly, holding each tone for (1) FOUR counts and (2) EIGHT counts.
When playing long tones, practice (1) ◁— and (2) ◁——▷.

SLURS

Also practice very slowly, holding each tone of each slur for FOUR counts.

164

INTRODUCING "MIDDLE D#"

165

THEME from ZAMPA

Moderato   HEROLD

166

MENUET from SYMPHONY

Leggiero   MOZART

167

914-103

THE FIRST NOEL

Traditional

STRENGTHENING "HIGH G#"

Barcarolle from Tales of Hoffmann

OFFENBACH

Chromatic Scale

Also practice very slowly, holding each tone for EIGHT counts.
When playing long tones practice (1) $\longleftarrow$ and (2) $\longleftarrow$ $\longrightarrow$.

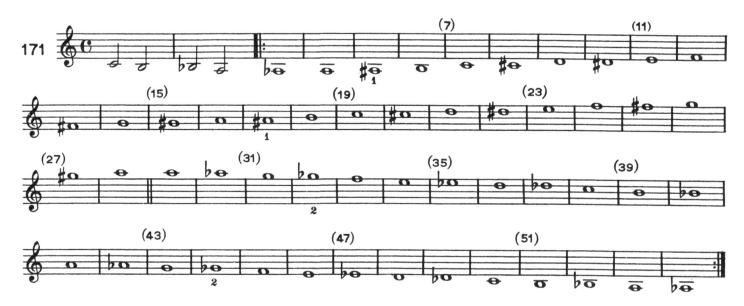

SHORT CHROMATIC STUDIES

Also practice very slowly, holding each tone for (1) FOUR counts and (2) EIGHT counts.
When playing long tones practice (1) $\longleftarrow$ and (2) $\longleftarrow$ $\longrightarrow$.

Also practice very legato, (1) slurring each two tones, and (2) slurring each four tones.

914-103

CHROMATIC EXERCISE

INTRODUCING "LOW G"

INTRODUCING "LOW F#" "(Gb)"

CHROMATIC EXERCISE IN THE LOW REGISTER

Also practice slowly, holding each tone for (1) TWO counts and (2) FOUR counts.

BASIC CHROMATIC STUDIES

Also practice tonguing each tone.

CHROMATIC EXERCISES IN TRIPLETS

Arban Foundation Studies

193

194

195

196

197

198

199

200

201

202

(9)

(17)

203

(9)

(17)

204

(9)

(17)

205

206

207

208

209

210

914-103

211

212

213

214

215

216

914-103

217

218

219

220

221

222

223

224

225

Interval Exercises

Also practice slowly, holding each tone for (1) TWO counts and (2) FOUR counts.

Octave Study

J.B. ARBAN

914-103

Arban Interval Slurs

(a) Also practice very slowly, holding each tone of each slur for FOUR counts.
(b) Also practice tonguing each note.

THIRDS

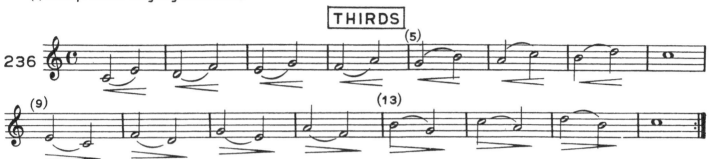

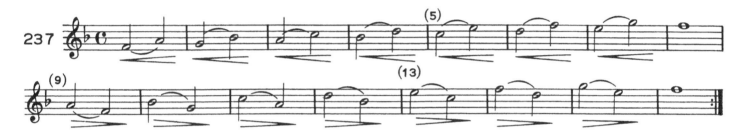

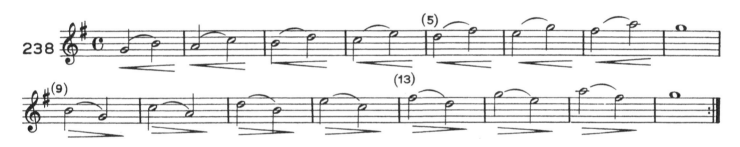

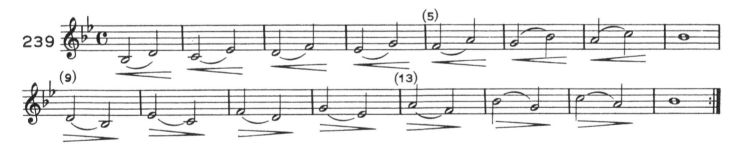

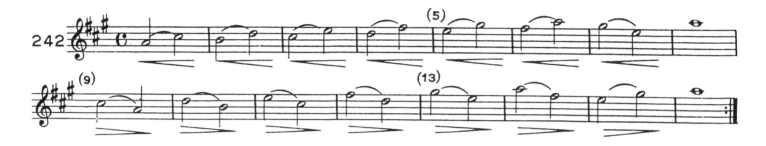

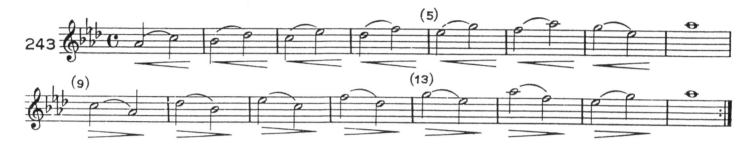

FOURTHS

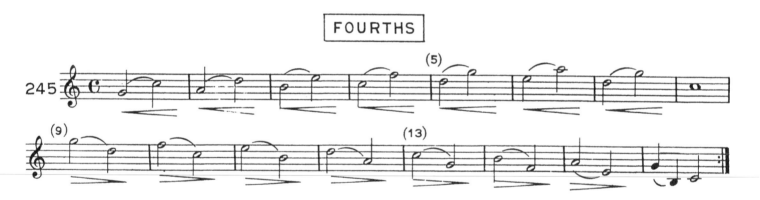

914-103

248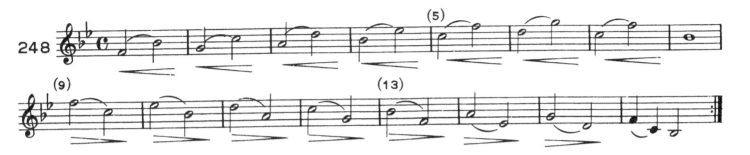

249

250

251

252

253

Arban Lip Slurs

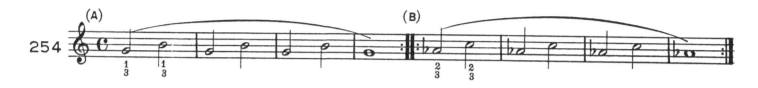

254

255

256

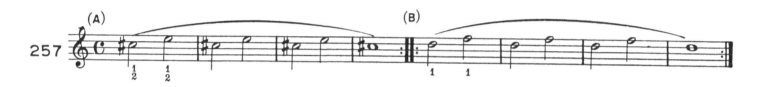

257

258

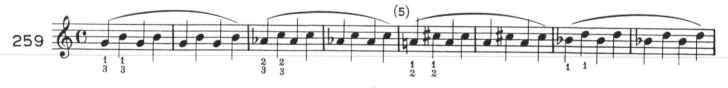

259

914-103

260

261

Count 1   2   3   4

Rhythmic Studies and Excerpts

Selected from the works of ARBAN, ST. JACOME and others

INTRODUCING SIXTEENTH NOTES

QUARTER AND SIXTEENTH NOTES ALTERNATED

FIERCE FLAMES ARE RAGING

from Il Trovatore

VERDI

RHYTHMICAL STUDY

ARBAN STUDY

FANFARE

914-103

RHYTHMICAL STUDY

EXCERPT from STRADELLA

Von FLOTOW

ARBAN STUDY

Also practice tonguing each note.

ROSA LEE

Southern Melody

INTRODUCING THE DOTTED EIGHTH NOTE FOLLOWED BY A SIXTEENTH NOTE

ARBAN STUDY

LA CZARINE

GANNE

HAIL! HAIL! THE GANGS ALL HERE
from The Pirates of Penzance

Sir ARTHUR SULLIVAN

PRESIDENT'S MARCH

Based on a Scotch Air

914-103

TRIPLETS

282 Count 1   2   3   4

QUARTER NOTES AND TRIPLETS ALTERNATED

283

PILGRIMS' CHORUS
from Tannhauser

WAGNER

Maestoso

284

(9)   (13)

ANDANTE
from Fifth Symphony

TSCHAIKOWSKY

Con amore

285

(9)   (13)

SOLDIERS' CHORUS
from Faust

GOUNOD

Grandioso

286

(9)

(13)

914-103

TRIPLET EXERCISE

ST. JACOME

287

SCENES THAT ARE BRIGHTEST
from Maritana

WALLACE

288

THEME from THE CORONATION MARCH

MEYERBEER

289

CHORD STUDY

ST. JACOME

290

EXCERPT from HULDIGUNGSMARCH

GRIEG

291

INTRODUCING SYNCOPATION

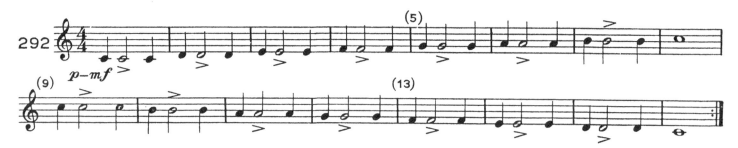

FINALE, Second Act of ZAMPA

HEROLD

THE SIXTEENTH NOTE FOLLOWED BY A DOTTED EIGHTH NOTE

SWING LOW, SWEET CHARIOT

HARRY T. BURLEIGH

TANGO

ALBENIZ

At this stage of advancement the student should, in addition to continuing his study of MODERN ARBAN - ST. JACOME in a systematic fashion, turn to MODERN PARES FOUNDATION STUDIES FOR CORNET(published by Rubank, Inc.) a companion volume to the present work, and begin at once the all important procedure of daily scale practice.

St. Jacome Articulation Studies

Articulations to be played.

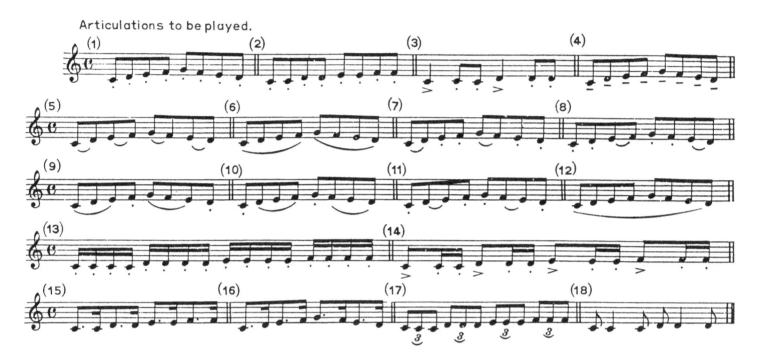

304

305

306

307

308

309

St. Jacome Lip Exercises

OPEN TONE STUDIES

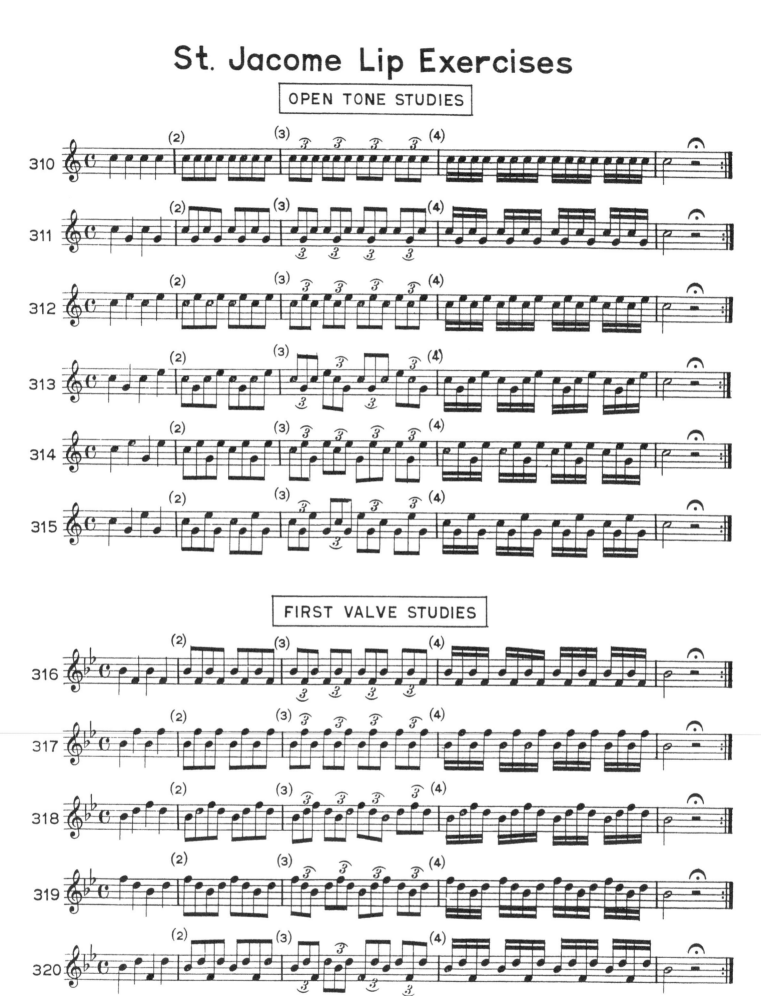

FIRST VALVE STUDIES

Major Scales in Thirds

Articulations to be played.

Also practice very slowly, holding each tone for (1) FOUR counts and (2) EIGHT counts.
When playing long tones, practice (1) ‹< and (2) ‹< >

Basic Lip Slurs

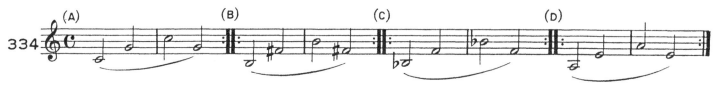

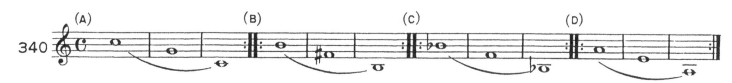

914-103

342

343

344

345

346

347

348

349

350

351 Use 1st and 3rd valves only.

352 Use 1st and 3rd valves only.

353 Use 1st and 3rd valves only.

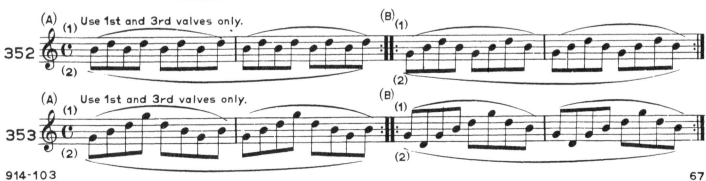

Introducing Alla Breve (Cut) Time

Alla Breve (Cut) Time is 4/4 Time (Meter) with TWO BEATS to the measure instead of four.
It is indicated by the sign ₵.

914-103

Cornet (Trumpet) Duets*

Selected from the works of ARBAN, ST. JACOME, CARNAUD and others.

FIRST DUET IN COMMON OR ALLA BREVE TIME

(Before playing duets in Alla Breve Time, carefully
study this procedure as illustrated on page 68.)

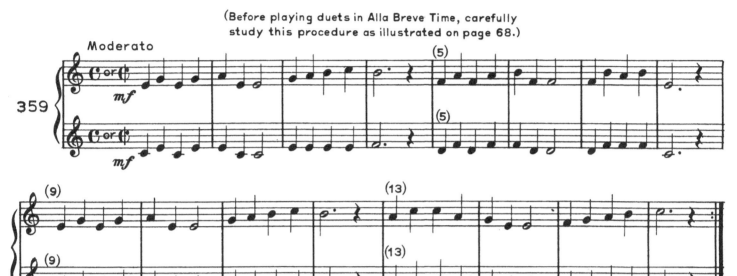

WALTZ IN DUET STYLE

Von BLON

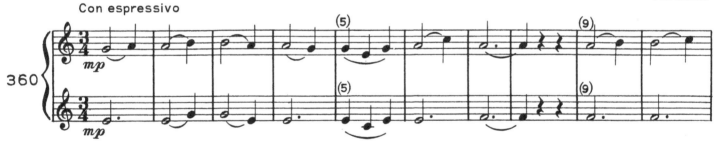

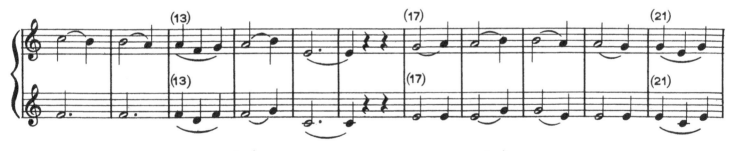

* For additional material the "Selected Duets for Cornet or Trumpet, Vol. I," by H. Voxman (Rubank) is highly recommended.

SECOND DUET IN COMMON OR ALLA BREVE TIME

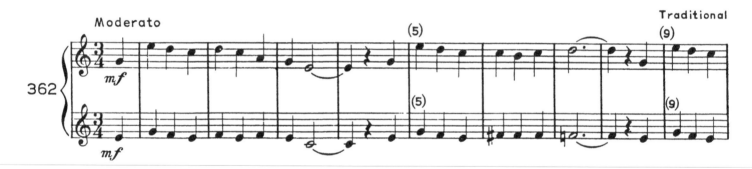

SCOTCH AIR

THIRD DUET IN COMMON OR ALLA BREVE TIME

CARNAUD

FAVORITE MELODY

J. WINNER

SILENT NIGHT

FRANZ GRUBER

TRADITIONAL DUET IN COMMON OR ALLA BREVE TIME

ST. JACOME

Andantino

366

Old Black Joe

STEPHEN C. FOSTER

Affetuosamente

367

914-103

RHYTHMICAL DUET IN COMMON OR ALLA BREVE TIME

ST. JACOME

ARTISTIC DUET

ST. JACOME

Just A Song at Twilight

MOLLOY

Londonderry Air

Traditional

914-103

Russian Hymn

Traditional

Maestoso

372

Viennese Melody

Traditional

Andantino

373

The Miller of the Dee

Traditional

Allégro ma non troppo

374

Auld Lang Syne

Scotch Folk Song

Con energico

375

914-103

Rondo

CARNAUD

Romance

REDOWA

377

L'Elisire D'Amore

DONIZETTI

378

914-103

THEME

BEETHOVEN

379

Carry Me Back to Old Virginny

JAMES A. BLAND

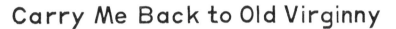

380

Allegro de Concert No.1

ST. JACOME

Brillante

381

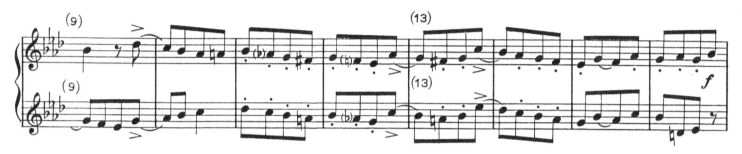

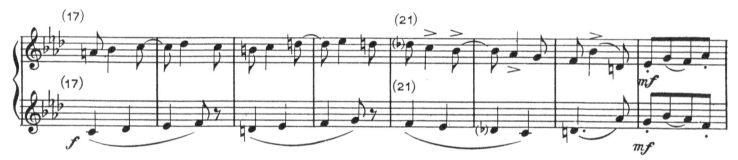

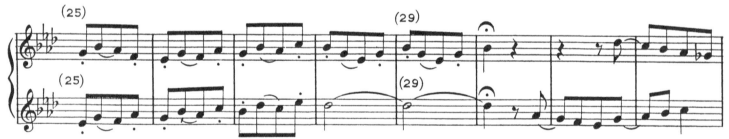

Allegro de Concert No.2

Con brio

ST. JACOME

382

Musical Embellishments (Ornamentation)

The Modern Grace Note (known theoretically as an ACCIACCATURA) is a small ornamental note written with a line through its stem. It is played quickly and its time value is taken from that of the note preceding it rather than from that of the note to which it is attached.

SINGLE GRACE NOTES

DOUBLE GRACE NOTES

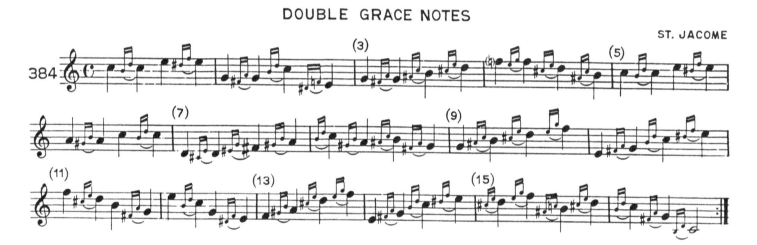

TRIPLE GRACE NOTES

The GRUPETTO (popularly known as a Turn) is a musical ornament consisting of a group of notes formed by taking the adjoining notes above and below the principal note, according to its position in the diatonic scale. It is indicated by the sign ∽ and is used in different ways.

ARBAN GRUPETTO STUDY No. 1

ARBAN GRUPETTO STUDY No. 2

The TRILL (sometimes called a Shake) is the most commonly used embellishment in music. It is an ornamental effect produced by the rapid and regular alterations of two tones, either a whole step or a half-step apart, and is indicated by the letters *tr* above the principal note, the alternate note being the one above it. It does not matter how many notes a trill contains; the greater the number of notes in a trill, the more life and brilliancy the embellishment will radiate.

388

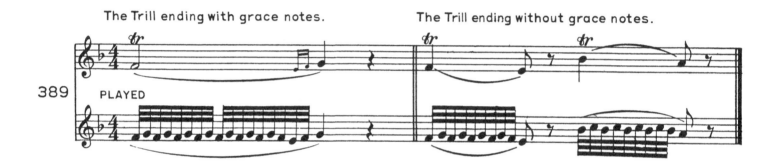

389

ARBAN TRILL ETUDE

390

84

914-103

St. Jacome Complete Table of Trills
(Basic Exercises)

E = Easy   D = Difficult   ⊕ = Hardly practicable

Practice each exercise many times.

Complete page 104 before practicing these exercises.

The MORDANT (sometimes called a Passing Shake) is, in its most commonly played form, a double grace note embellishment consisting of the principal note alternated with a note above it. The sign ∿ placed over a note indicates the mordant.

MORDANT STUDY

ST. JACOME EMBELLISHMENT ETUDE

914-103

Key of A Minor

(Relative to the Key of C Major)

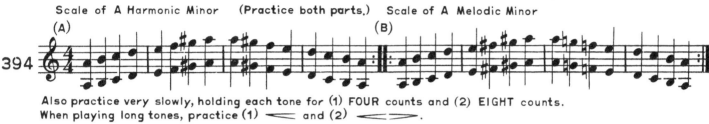

Scale of A Harmonic Minor   (Practice both parts.)   Scale of A Melodic Minor

394

Also practice very slowly, holding each tone for (1) FOUR counts and (2) EIGHT counts.
When playing long tones, practice (1) ⟨ and (2) ⟨⟩.

ST. JACOME ETUDE IN A MINOR

395

SONG OF THE VOLGA BOATMAN

Russian Folk Song

Con dolore

396

Key of D Minor

(Relative to the Key of F Major)

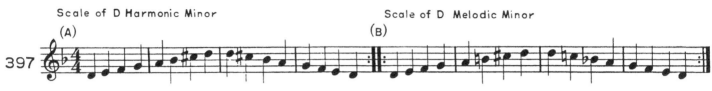

Scale of D Harmonic Minor   Scale of D Melodic Minor

Also practice very slowly, holding each tone for (1) FOUR counts and (2) EIGHT counts.
When playing long tones, practice (1) $\prec$ and (2) $\prec$ $\succ$

ST. JACOME ETUDE IN D MINOR

SERENADE

SCHUBERT

pp 914-103

Key of E Minor

(Relative to the Key of G Major)

Scale of E Harmonic Minor (A)   Scale of E Melodic Minor (B)

400

Also practice very slowly, holding each tone for (1) FOUR counts and (2) EIGHT counts.
When playing long tones, practice (1) ⟨ and (2) ⟨ ⟩

ST. JACOME ETUDE IN E MINOR

401

(5)

(9)   (13)

(17)

CHANSON TRISTE

TSCHAIKOWSKY

Doloroso   (5)

402   mp

(9)   (13)

(17)   (21)

(25)   (29)

rit.

Key of G Minor

(Relative to the Key of B♭ Major)

Scale of G Harmonic Minor (Practice both parts.)   Scale of G Melodic Minor

(A)   (B)

403

Also practice very slowly, holding each tone for (1) FOUR counts and (2) EIGHT counts.
When playing long tones, practice (1) ⟨ and (2) ⟨ ⟩.

ST. JACOME ETUDE IN G MINOR

404

(5)

(9)

(13)

ORIENTALE

CESAR CUI
Op. 50

Larghetto

405

(5)

(9)

(13)   (17)

(21)

(25)   (29)

(33)

Key of B Minor
(Relative to the Key of D Major)

Scale of B Harmonic Minor   Scale of B Melodic Minor

(A)   **(B)**

406

Also practice very slowly, holding each tone for (1) FOUR counts and (2) EIGHT counts.
When playing long tones, practice (1) ⟨ and (2) ⟨ ⟩

ST. JACOME ETUDE IN B MINOR

407

(5)   **(9)**

(13)

(17)

NIGHT WINDS

TSCHAIKOWSKY
Op. 30, No. 24

Agitato   **(5)**

408

(9)   **(13)**

(17)   **(21)**

(25)   **(29)**

Key of C Minor
(Relative to the Key of E♭ Major)

Scale of C Harmonic Minor

Scale of C Melodic Minor

409

Also practice very slowly, holding each tone for (1) FOUR counts and (2) EIGHT counts.
When playing long tones, practice (1) ⤙ and (2) ⤙⤚.

ST. JACOME ETUDE IN C MINOR

410

NATIVE HOMELAND

Con calore

Folk Song

411

mf

Key of F# Minor

(Relative to the Key of A Major)

Scale of F# Harmonic Minor   Scale of F# Melodic Minor

412

Also practice very slowly, holding each tone for (1) FOUR counts and (2) EIGHT counts.
When playing long tones, practice (1) ⏝ and (2) ⏝

ST. JACOME ETUDE IN F# MINOR

413

ELEGIE

MASSENET

414

Key of F Minor

(Relative to the Key of A♭ Major)

Scale of F Harmonic Minor

Scale of F Melodic Minor

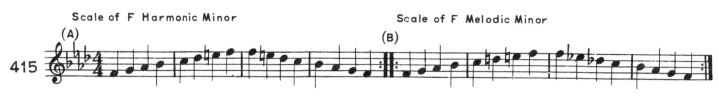

415

Also practice very slowly, holding each tone for (1) FOUR counts and (2) EIGHT counts.
When playing long tones, practice (1) ◁ and (2) ◁ ▷

ST. JACOME ETUDE IN F MINOR

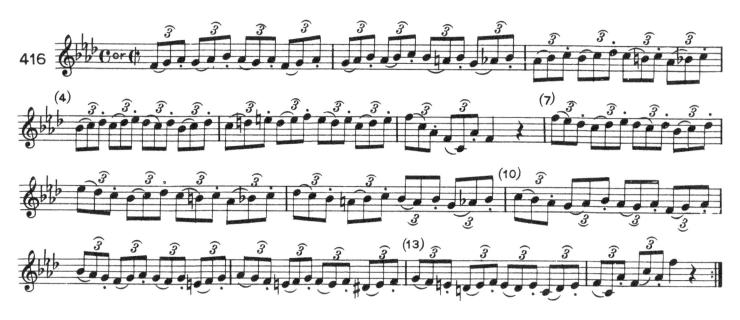

416

MAZURKA

J. LEYBACH

Ben marcato

417

Key of C# Minor

(Relative to the Key of E Major)

Scale of C# Harmonic Minor

Scale of C# Melodic Minor

(A) **(B)**

418

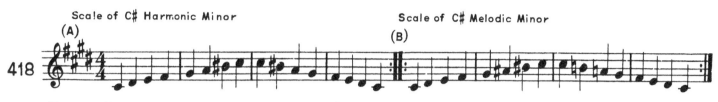

Also practice very slowly, holding each tone for (1) FOUR counts and (2) EIGHT counts.
When playing long tones, practice (1) ⟨ and (2) ⟨ ⟩.

ST. JACOME ETUDE IN C# MINOR

419

BOLERO

J. LEYBACH

Allegro

420

mf

St. Jacome Advanced Interval Slurs

FIFTHS and SIXTHS

Practice slowly. Also practice tonguing each note.

SIXTHS and SEVENTHS

OCTAVES

St. Jacome Chromatic Studies

SCALE EXERCISE

Practice in both Common and Alla Breve time.

INTERVAL EXERCISE

Practice in both Common and Alla Breve time.
Also practice (1) slurring each TWO tones, (2) slurring each FOUR tones, and (3) slurring each EIGHT tones.

Triple Tonguing

426

ta ta ka ta ta ka ta
tu tu ku tu tu ku tu

427

ta ta ka ta ta ka ta ta ka ta
tu tu ku tu tu ku tu tu ku tu

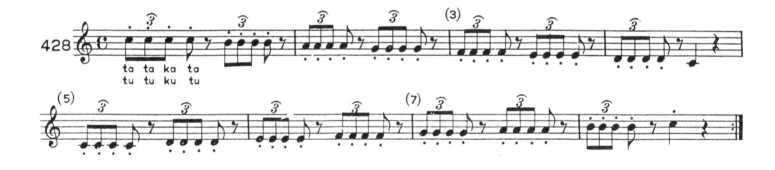

428

ta ta ka ta
tu tu ku tu

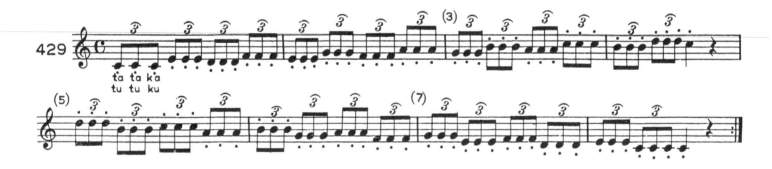

429

ta ta ka
tu tu ku

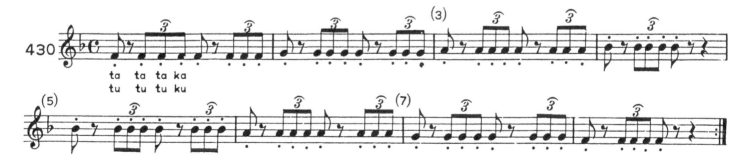

430

ta ta ta ka
tu tu tu ku

Triple Tongue Patterns
To be practiced on St. Jacome Articulation
Studies (No's. 301, 302, 303, 304, 305, 306, 307, 308, 309), Pages 62-63.

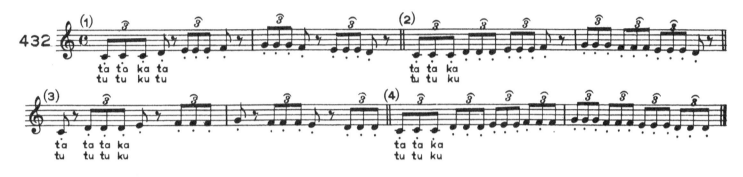

Polka Brilliant
from La Fille de Madam Angot

J. LEYBACH
Op.169

Double Tonguing

Double Tongue Patterns

To be practiced on St. Jacome Articulation
Studies (No's. 301, 302, 303, 304, 305, 306, 307, 308, 309), Pages 62-63.

Major and Minor Scales with Basic Articulations

SINGLE TONGUE ARTICULATIONS

Practice single tongue articulations in both Common and Alla Breve time.

TRIPLE TONGUE ARTICULATIONS

DOUBLE TONGUE ARTICULATIONS

MAJOR and MINOR SCALES

C Major

A Harmonic Minor (Practice both parts)

A Melodic Minor (Practice both parts)

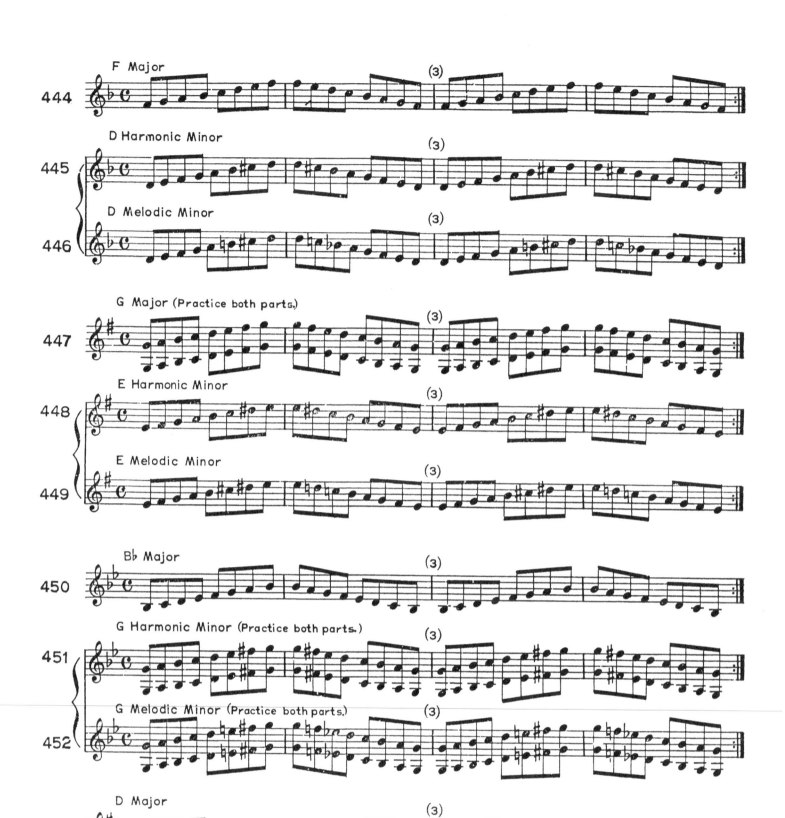

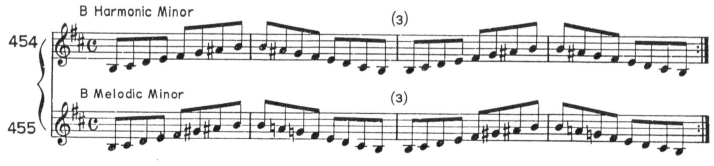

Developing High B♭, B and C

"HIGH B♭"

"HIGH B"

"HIGH C"

STRENGTHENING HIGH TONES

Scale of B♭ Major

Scale of C Major

For follow-up material use the Rubank "Advanced Method for Cornet or Trumpet, Vol. II" (Voxman-Gower), and the "Selected Studies for Cornet or Trumpet" (Voxman).